Into the Abyss

INTO THE ABYSS

the Poetry of

GARY K. FARLOW

A.B.O. Comix
Oakland CA

The A.B.O. Comix Collective is sustained by volunteers, community donations, grant funding, and various daring bank heists. It is also sustained by the perseverance, bravery, kindness, empathy, and love that our contributors share with us.

This book was published with the generous support of The Mellon Foundation.

May this book be a pathway out of the Abyss.

Edited by Brett Tomás Gonzalez, Casper Cendre, and Kaia Ball.

Library of Congress Control Number: 2026937242
ISBN-13: 978-1-961682-12-2

If you are currently incarcerated and would like a copy of this book or our catalogue, please write to us!

P.O. Box 11584, Oakland CA 94611
www.abocomix.org

DEDICATIONS

To Anthony, the love of my life:

To Sandra and Althea, my guardian angels:

To my brother Harold, who always believed in me:

To Andre, Josh, and Carolyn, you epitomize true friendship:

To Lewis and Chris, without whom you would not be reading this

People will die,
flowers will wilt,
steel will break,
but-
Hope can endure,
Even in the darkest places...

TABLE OF CONTENTS

Justice is the first virtue of social institutions ...
John Rawls (1921-2002)

No free man shall be imprisoned, except by the law of the land.
Barons of King John (13th Century)

There is nothing to take a man's freedom away from him, save other men.
Ayn Rand (1905-1982)

Nothing can truly prepare a man for prison. There are no guidebooks, no navigation system, no method that is universal. It is trial (no pun intended) and error.

When I was paroled on July 16, 2021, by the North Carolina Parole Commission, after having served 30 years on an 80-year sentence, I thought that my nightmare had at last come to an end. Then I was told that, no, I would not be going home but was being sent to South Carolina to serve a consecutive 15-year sentence for the same crime and victim as in North Carolina. Southern Justice!

I cannot begin to describe my emotions that day. It was, upon arrival at the SCDC Kirkland Reception and Evaluation Center in Columbia, that the shock, the deja vu, the "Groundhog Day" movie feeling of having to once more plunge into the abyss of a prison system set in. The difference this time was that I was no longer a young, healthy 31-year-old like I was in 1991 when I began my NC prison sentence. Now, I was 63 years old with many chronic health conditions and had no one-no family, friends, or support in this state.

So here I was, a 63-year-old legally blind inmate already risk assessed as being a "Minimal risk of re-arrest" beginning all over once more.

Prison can be a muse for the poet. It has inspired great writers like Alexander Solsynitszin, Oscar Wilde, O'Henry (William S. Porter).

Prison has fueled the quest for equality and civil rights-who can forget the Rev. Dr. Martin Luther King, Jr.'s "Letter from the Birmingham Jail" or Nelson Mandela's "Long Way Home"? So, too, has prison provided me with material to practice my craft of poetry.

This collection of poems focuses on my sojourn in the South Carolina Department of Corrections. It is, as my poetry will portray, a prison system of truly incomprehensible contradictions, violence, senseless cruelty on the part of the staff and inmates, and utter chaos. While prison is not intended to be a vacation or a pleasant experience, it is a sad commentary on our nation's position as a "leader of the free world" that 2.2 million Americans are housed in correctional facilities. One out of every three Americans have seen the inside of a prison or jail. The United States ranks third in human history having such a huge percentage of its citizens behind the wire-behind only Stalinist Russia and Hitler's Germany. Not a very attractive company!

Poetry, like many forms of art, can convey the deep emotions which dwell in each of us. Poems can trigger a memory, a feeling, return the reader to a forgotten moment in time. Poetry can rekindle buried feelings, heal pain, and protest our inhumanity to one another. Be it civil rights, war, or prison, poetry can be a vehicle for addressing social issues. As I write in one poem, "life isn't all rainbows and butterflies, for you cannot change the mind until you touch the heart."

So it is, in our "Land of Liberty," we have a judicial and penal system that is "the best that money can buy," leaving the poor, the marginalized, without true justice.

The poetry in this collection may shock the reader into saying, "surely that can't be true! Not in America!" Let me assure you that every poem contained in this collection was penned as the events they describe unfolded, not in hindsight but as it took place.

I hope that the well-meaning intentions of the New England Quakers, who developed America's first penal system, one that is now a muti-billion-dollar industry, will be recognized as an idea long past its expiration date. Prison, as a remedy and deterrent to crime, simply does not work. Poetry does. Read on and discover how poetry expresses man's invention of inhumanity, this bit of purgatory on earth called prison. Come with me *Into the Abyss*.

Gary K. Farlow

INTO THE ABYSS

PRISON

Beautifully brutal,
Painfully bittersweet.
Emotions raw, real, deep,
Inside the walls,
Inside the man,
Gritty, graceful,
Like being in limbo,
Tears, laughter,
Life, death,
Captive, free,
Light, darkness,
Hope shines,
From the inside out.

Table of Contents

My mother's tears in court.
Numbness, emptiness.
Finally - acceptance.
Liberation, to be me ...
Senior citizen, page 65,
A time of reflection,
Retrospect.
Teaching, writing,
Finding love at last,
love for myself,
love for another,
Peace, the return of hope
Awaiting freedom.

WHAT THESE WALLS CANNOT HOLD

It is an extraordinary thing
To meet someone
You can marry your soul to
And who accepts you
For who you are.
I've waited for years
To hear a song.
My heart opens to your voice
Like the flowers
To the kiss of dawn.
Your touch has words
That speak to me,
Every syllable sweet.
Your love is a rainbow
That appears
When thoughts of you
Dry my tears.
Your tenderness
Bankrupts the English language.
For what is the color of love?
The sky is blue,
The grass is green,
Your heart is golden,
Radiant like the sun.
Your lips sweet,
Like a red rose.
Your tears pure,
Like crystal water.
What good is love
If it cannot be expressed?

If one has no interest
In love,
What is the point
Of life?
To love you
Is to risk loss,
But dwell in the hope,
The belief,
We shall rise
Above these walls...
Together.

Eternal Shadows

I pass through the vapor of breaths
Bitter, like disappointment.
Holding fast, remembering.
Without darkness
Nothing is born.
Feeling lost, like a package
Whose shipping label
Has been torn off.
We are freeze-framed
At our moment of shame.
But I give no counsel
To the darkness
That surrounds me.
My tenacity
Tunnels under enemy lines
Planting mine fields
Of compassion,
Belief, strength,
Willpower, unity.
Replacing prejudice,
Hate, and intolerance.
Life is not determined
By where we are
On the outside,
Bitter like acid rain,
Existing between the bonds
Of hope and shame.

PRELUDE TO A RIOT

It began as a result
of a seemingly trivial matter,
the phones are out
mail isn't delivered
visitation is cancelled
chow is late
the rec yard is closed
the commissary computer is down

Words begin to flow,
one bumps into another,
a guard yells lockdown
one shove, then another
a punch is thrown
melee ensues
whistles are blown
sirens blare

Chaos and destruction
reign from cellblock to cellblock,
homemade knives are brandished
blood is spilt
innocents are not spared
elderly cannot escape
old grudges are settled
pain and death

This is the possibility
that an inmate faces daily,
always on alert

prepared for battle
unable to show fear.
When will it come?
Will it come?
This is life in a U.S. prison.

Pledge of Allegiance

Here in the land of cotton
Where the first shot was fired
that would see more American blood
than any other conflict
We sit in darkness;
Images of freedom and loved ones
swirling into a miasma of pain,
the intercom buzzes
reciting the Pledge of Allegiance daily
"With liberty and justice for all"?
Our liberty is two five-minute phone calls
and a shower thrice weekly.
Otherwise, it's twenty-four lockdown,
three people packed into every 7 x 9 cell,
"And to the Republic for which it stands,"
this is our republic,
with shades of Abu Ghraib and injustice for all,
as water slowly drips down the cinderblock wall
every time a toilet upstairs is flushed,
the cell reeking of urine and humanity
while the intercom urges personal hygiene
and keeping the cell sanitized.
"One nation"? "Under God"?
Don't make me laugh...or cry.

THE DESERT

In this desert called prison
I turn toward the emptiness,
Fearing the self, fleeing the past.

I stand alone,
Asking no one's help.
Bereft,
As I quiet racing thoughts
And the bondage of my past.

I once clung to the world,
Endeavoring to possess
Consumed by a thirst,
Insatiable.

Now I dwell alone
Yet surrounded
By the haunted specters
Of thousands
Who drink from the well of sorrow,
Unable to kindle the fire of love
With the twigs of passion.

Here I dwell, alone,
In the desert called prison.

Countdown

Its been 4 hours since my last meal
a Styrofoam tray with yellow grits
a slice of bologna
and two slices of stale bread

Its been 6 hours since I last ate
my world reduced to one window
as I watch night fade to day
then back again

Its been 10 hours since I last ate
nearly 3 months since I smelled fresh air
Felt the sun
or could walk beyond my 7 x 9 world

Its been 12 hours since I last ate
the relentless ticking of my watch
the only measure of time
as life passes utterly unnoticed

Its been 15 hours since my last meal
the days divided by meals
except on weekends when its only 2 meals
the portions miniscule, and always cold

And here is the food cart
and soon it will be the countdown
until it's time to eat again
as my watch ticks on

Four Walls

Four walls have held me captive

For strong, high walls

Right and wrong

Shall and shall not

If for a moment I had

Samson's strength

I'd shove these walls far back

Free I'd be

To roam and ramble

Going, doing, being

Would it be a happy state?

I might fear freedom

After all, these four walls

Have defined my world

Have held me so long

They pen me in

From a world

Full of those

Who have judged me

Yet do not know me

I am more than the sum

Of my past

Only A Dream

Up in the air and over the wire,

My feet touch the frosted grass,

Or is it summer and dew is sweet?

Scents assail me as I wander

The spice of autumn,

The fragrance of spring,

The crispness of winter.

I am a kaleidoscope of sensations.

Leaves whisper my name

In the newness of April,

In the bursting colors of October.

A creek gurgles by its banks,

The water refreshing in July,

Icy in January.

Life sustaining year around.

A klaxon blares,

"Five minutes til count!"

And I am back again.

It was all just a dream.

Effigy

What's happened?

Where is my life?

I don't understand.

Surrounded by violence

As I sink deeper into despair.

No resolution in sight;

Harassment, pain.

Tirades of intimidation

Of millions in bondage

Like tropical vines tangling

And imprisoning the very soul.

Questioning forbidden.

Dreams crushed.

Hopes shattered.

Tormentors masquerading

As law and order

But like jungle felines

Shredding my soul

In the wilderness of negativity,

Prejudice, hate.

I trudge a path of twisting

Riotous turns.

Lost, like a package

With a missing label.

I pass through the vapor of breaths

The Bird

Maya Angelou's caged bird does not sing,
it wails, screaming for redemption,
to a nation, a society, that turns its back,
eyes closed, and deaf ears to the caged.

Prisoners we both are, the bird and I,
at the hands of man, captives
like the exhibits in a zoo,
oddities, separated from the world;

The bird's gilded cage and my iron bars
are different, yet the same;
The bird may experience a certain care
A tenderness, even love;

The inmate seldom knows such,
amidst whistles and blaring horns,
a cacophony of prisoner and captor,
the daily chaos of prison;

I know how the caged bird feels,
and it does not sing, it cries,
looking between the bars at freedom,
just as I stand at my barred window.

Into The Abyss

This place is called Reception and Evaluation
as if you're a valued guest
at a posh resort hotel or perhaps
a Tony California clinic.

In reality, its more like Retribution and Emasculation
Rejection and Elimination
Refuse and Erasure.

Here, in this hotel of the damned
Revulsion and Entanglement
Riddance and Entrapment.

The Reception is unsmiling
The Evaluation perfunctory

Here we sit, day in, day out
Robbed and Excommunicated
Ridiculed and Emaciated

In this world of the Reviled and Embittered
Toto, I don't think we are in Kansas anymore.

 Gary K. Farlow

Bus Ride

We are awakened at 3 am
bodies slouching
eyes full of sleep
we shuffle out...fresh air!
Harassed and yelled at by guards
"Tuck that shirt in!"
"Stand straight!"
"Eyes to the front I"
"No talking!"
The halogen lights cast eerie shadows
no one makes eye contact
peanut butter and crackers for breakfast
ten minutes to eat...nothing to drink
We move out
Each bus holds sixty-five
a convoy of packed sardines
in an oil of anxiety
the cuffs are clenched tight
This is called "diesel therapy"
We pull out onto the highway
morning commuters pass us by
Wonder what they had for breakfast?
You, in the red Honda,
do you know how precious your freedom is?
Will that ever be me?

Pedagogy of the Oppressed

A personal Holocaust, prison.
The absence of reason.
How can I endure this encampment?
Forsaken in an abyss.
The utter isolation of despair.
Sheer darkness bringing attacks
Of abject misery.
I am a walking cadaver of
My former self.
None to understand or look
Beyond my mask.
Within the depths of hell,
Prison, a terrifying place.
Consumed in the very bowels
Of humanity.
A monstrous place, prison.
My soul's murdered spirit
Encumbered in chains of secrecy.
This journey with seemingly
No end.
How much longer?

Evolution of a Dixiecrat

Ban abortion?

Check.

Separate but equal?

Check.

Tough on crime?

Check.

Reduce welfare?

Check.

Nuclear armament?

Check.

Stop immigration?

Check.

This court finds you guilty.

Check.

You are hereby sentenced to 80 years.

Check.

Ruined reputation.

Check.

Convicted felon.

Check.

Forever branded.

Check.

The shoe is now on the other foot.

Check.

The fruit of my labors.

Check mate.

WHAT IS THE COLOR OF JUSTICE?

Can I leave a painful past?
Ever vigil for verbal assaults.
No warning, I live like a
Prisoner of war.
My days traversing a
Minefield.
My youth, a pawn
Of belittlement and shame.
A hopeless existence
With no illusions of parole.
No Walton's or Cleavers.
A loving family fading into
Heartless misery.
Immobilized. Alone.
A lack of security.
My grief, my love,
With nowhere to go.
For I have been a Dismas,
Hanging, reviled.
A Magdalene,
Waiting outside a tomb.
A disciple,
Frightened, scattered.
A blind man, a leper, a lame.
There will be no forgiveness,
No resurrection.
There are no second acts
In this theatre of the absurd
Called American life.

Gary K. Farlow

We simply bury
What we fear the most.
The silence is where
We hide our shame.

QUARANTINE

The intercom buzzes to life
"Remember to maintain personal hygiene
and wash your hands and keep
your cell clean"
but its been seven days since I last had a shower
and we never receive cleaning supplies

We are told multiple times daily
"Wear your mask at all times,
observe social distancing,
and avoid contact"
Yet, guards move among us daily, unmasked while
we are crammed three in a cell built for one.

The intercom buzzes again
"If you haven't received your Covid vaccination
please fill out a sick call request
and submit it today"
Yet, sick calls go unanswered and the latest outbreak
was brought in by a guard-they refuse vaccination

The quarantine continues and this revolution
is far too sad to be televised.

LOCKDOWN

It is late summer
The grass is green
And I long to feel
The sun on my face.

The grass is green
As I press against the window
The sun on my face
While clouds begin to gather.

As I press against the window
A raindrop splatters on the grass
While clouds begin to gather
And the sun fades into darkness

A raindrop splatters on the glass
I think of how long I've been inside these walls
And the sun fades to darkness
Like my life slowly slipping away

I think of how long I've been inside these walls
Losing touch, bit by bit
Like my life slowly slipping away
In this Southern cinderblock hell.

Mail

Time for mail delivery
as I tense
anxiously awaiting
eyes riveted
to the slot beneath the door

I hear the footsteps
as the guard passes
and I deflate
like a spent party balloon
Forgotten, out of mind

Do you know how it feels
to spend your day waiting
in silent hope
for that one moment
when life becomes bearable

But not today
as I lay down
curling into myself
quiet tears flowing
to await mail delivery tomorrow

My name is Andre

Hello. Welcome.
His voice was soft, almost melodic
Once could imagine such a voice
lulling a person in a warm cocoon
But he was here, in this land of the brutal
to promote peace.
My name is Andre.
Welcome to Mindful Meditation.
For twelve weeks we met
Twenty-four convicts of various crimes
coming together to develop compassion.
Undaunted by this ominous task
Andre came each Friday
bearing a smile, that voice of silk,
and compassion for the unlovable.
I've heard that into each life
will come a brief encounter
A person known for only a short time
but their impact is so profound
you are left forever changed.
Andre never tried to proselytize
Yet his "stealth Buddhism"
imparted kindness, tolerance, hope,
replacing mistrust, bigotry, and anguish.
I shall never forget him.

Midnight Meow

They square off, eye to eye
unblinking in the dance
of ancient warriors
since time immemorial
One advances, one retreats
but the challenge continues
Until one blinks
and scampers away
The victor lets go a howl
of feline triumph
Tell me if you can
who is the more
civilized
them or us?

Gary K. Farlow

The Cats

Do they know they are in prison?
These feline beasts who prowl the yard
As we sit captive in a cell,
They have the run of the grounds
The freedom to come and go at will
Yet, they stay
Fed by staff and kitchen workers
They fare better than we
For they have committed no crime
And society condemns them not
Yet, they stay
Surrounded by barbed-wire
And gun-toting goons
Tobacco dribbling from the corners of their mouths
They have never lived so well
These feline beasts who are blissfully
Unaware that they are in prison
A place built by man to separate man
To condemn man while they run free.

Let It Rain

I know you've heard it
that one piece of sinister advice
cheerfully given and meant
to propel you towards your goal
But...follow your own path
Sprinting towards compassion
Crawling towards judgement
Spreading your wings to soar
not forgetting to offer
a feather to another
still struggling to fly
Rejoicing in the rains
For you can't have a rainbow
Without a storm
and a saint is just a sinner
who got back up again
So, I will wait, like a beggar
holding fast to hope
Waiting for love and redemption to rise
and rain down upon us to quench
a draught-stricken world

Unchained

Whatever you are chained to
Jesus has come to set you free
Whatever piece of the past you hold tight to
There is a Savior who paid the debt to let you go
Whatever you are used to being defined by
The Son of God has come to set the record straight
What are you chained to?
Are you chained to who you used to be?
The thing you did, the habits you had?
Things you have no desire to admit?
Do you dwell in a prison of secrets? Of shame?
The things people once did to you?
Memories of those who once misused their power
and said or did terrible things to you
Things that broke your heart
but they placed all the blame on you
Do you live in a prison of abuse? Of self hate?
Chained to others expectations of you?
Do you dwell in a prison of never feeling worthy,
not good enough, no matter what you do?
Are you chained to a religion? A man-made
list of do's and don'ts you are told to live by
What are you chained to?
Jesus is not a policeman. He is your friend
He came, died, arose to unchain us all
So let your chains fall to the ground and let the
metal echo around the world-you are free!

WHAT'S IN A NAME?

Paris, who had never been to France,
Bone Crusher, who had never hit another human being,
Crowbar, who used one to murder twelve people,
Professor, who didn't finish high school,
Z, who dreamed of owning a Datsun,
Strawberry, who despised his given name of Walter,
Big Mo, who had a heart of gold,
Chante', who wanted to be America's Next Top Model,
September, who loved the Autumn,
Big E, who bore the uncanny resemblance to Mr. T,
Dove, who was so named by 1960's love children parents,
Rabbit, who was scared of his own shadow,
Cat Man, who was an inmate version of a crazy cat lady,
Capone, who fancied himself a Mafia king-pin,
"Johnny Cochrane," who was an "inmate lawyer,"
Brother Bill, who was everyone's friend,
Chemo, who wanted to be a scientist,
Tiny, who, at over 300 lbs., was anything but,
Disco, who once loved to strut his stuff,
Prophet, who swore he could foresee the future,
Buck, who was famous for making "buck," or inmate wine,
Pappa Smurf, who once was the oldest state prisoner,
Goat, who has made love to one,
Eddie Muster, who made love in funeral home with, well, ...
And all the countless "Jerseys," "Phillys," "Calis," "New Yorks,"
"Preachers," "D.C.s," "and "Cowboys."
What's in a name?
You just can never tell.

A LETTER TO AMERICA
ON THE DANGER OF COMPLACENCY

Why do you keep silent America?
Why do you keep your counsel as
millions of your citizens languish?
Why are you content to spend your taxes
to subsidize a failed system called prison?
Why America do you turn a blind eye, a deaf ear
to the cries for mercy, the plight of so many?
Why are you content to keep company with the
likes of Hitler and Stalin who also imprisoned millions?
Why America, do you refuse to speak out?
Is it because such an injustice hasn't been
Visited upon your doorstep---yet?
Is it due to your own feelings of moral
superiority over the less affluent?
Is it owed to your feelings of righteous
indignation towards crime rates---but,
are not those rates dropping?
Take care America. For as Bonhoeffer
wrote, your failure to speak out could
result in your own injustice---

and there will be no one left to speak out.

CHANT

When are we gonna get justice?

Innocent blood spilling in the street.

When are we gonna get justice?

Poisons put in the food we eat.

When are we gonna get justice?

Time to pull down the ivory tower.

When are we gonna get justice?

A new Jim Crow not meant to be.

When are we gonna get justice?

Is this what our Founding Fathers wanted to see?

When are we gonna get justice?

World make way for a wave of resistance.

When are we gonna get justice?

Let's be united brothers and sisters!

When are we gonna get justice?

Our quest for freedom is far from done.

When are we gonna get justice?

We won't stop til we are all One!

We won't stop until we get justice!

WHAT TIME IS IT IN PARADISE?

Here in this chamber of hell,
Filled with dreamers and the forlorn,
I am now a part of forever,
Just as it is a part of me now.
Dark living.
Half purgatory, half paradise,
Half light.
Have you ever been there?
Picasso said anything you can imagine
Is real.
Meaning and a shared imagination
Between artist and viewer,
Between poet and reader.
Here we interact with the imaginary,
Because the reality of what is causes
Us to create new realities.
Is it all a dream?
In this gloaming seclusion
From all that is,
The shadows and murk
Form our new what is...

Just Outside Charleston

Named after great rivers important and legendary,
Edisto, Wando, Ashley, Cooper,
these names also identify prison cellblocks
just 32 miles from Charleston's historic center,
but a world away from those genteel streets;
Instead of cobblestones and antebellum architecture
there are ugly, utilitarian structures some claim
look like a college, but a college for the damned,
prefab buildings and asphalt
Instead of graceful public squares and gardens,
barbed-wire instead of colonial era iron railing,
guard towers replace the vista of church spires,
golfcarts ferry officers on the grounds and not
the historic clop of horse-drawn carriages;
Inmates in stripes instead of brightly clad tourists,
the smell of institutional food assaults the senses
and not the famous low-country cuisine;
You cannot mistake one for the other
Just as Dorothy knew Oz wasn't Kansas,
there are no quaint inns here,
but it does house overnight guests who
like the Hotel California, check in but
seldom, if ever, will they check out;
For this is a man-made purgatory
Just 32 miles from the Holy City.

Wateree Prison

Like a relic from the antebellum South
stands a prison-Wateree
Down a drive of stately oaks
past the white-columned house
Home now to the warden and his family
where once the master dwelled
Now served by white-jacketed inmates
today's legal slavery
Where once horses were kept
inmates live in stalls turned into cells
They toil fields and tend cattle
just as in the Old South of long ago
But...was it really so long ago?
or has Jim Crow gone underground?
Disguised now in penitentiary stripes
in a state that observes Confederate Memorial Day
Fed a subsistent diet
paid no wages just as in days of yore
Solomon was right -
there is nothing new under the sun
especially in Dixie

Desire can destroy you

Gratitude is the cure for despair

Respect is a universal currency

Patience and joy are the antidotes

        for an ailing world

Hard work and honesty will always be

        rewarded in life

Heartbreaks of the past must be acknowledged

        if true healing is to occur

The hardest person to love is often oneself

Hope is a sure way to overcome failure

Build a fortune one small harvest at a time

Yesterday's ignorance is today's arrogance

I can accept failure, I will never accept

        not trying

Adversity begets opportunity and each new

        day brings both

In a world that feels is all too much trouble

        be the ocean of kindness

Grief will consume you
    trying to capture that which was lost
    leaving you spinning in sorrow
    in a fruitless pursuit of what was

Guilt can weigh upon you
    like the sultry humidity of a Southern summer
    a blanket of turmoil and self-hate
    carrying the luggage of pain through the airport of life

Grudges absorb your creativity
    in what is the most worthless of all causes
    trauma, perceived or real, becomes a noose
    strangling all positive energy

Cast off these consumers of life
    rise from the rubble of the past
    with the will of a Phoenix
    lifting from the ashes

Rise with the possibility of new found wings
    a reality more real than the debris
    for suffering never knocks
    seeking permission to enter

So view life like the back of a tapestry
    all the knots and tangles your adversities
    that once turned over become the beautiful
    priceless work of art that is...you

Butterfly

In the beginning...

It was all darkness and fear

I saw no way out

No end to anguish

A place that conveys death

Yet, can offer life?

To become new

I went into a cocoon

the target of transformation

that moment out in the darkness

became a metamorphosis

death and life working together

to bring about a beautiful new creation

from the darkness and dreariness

like a butterfly to emerge

forever changed

A person completely altered

But the world, this life

Isn't all rainbows and butterflies

You cannot change the mind

of anyone whose heart

has not been touched

Gary K. Farlow

Rainbow

A rainbow arcs above the razor wire
droplets of rain reflecting the sun
like Tiffany glass...
Red is the color of frustration
lost in this labyrinth
of stifled dreams...
Blue is the color of acceptance
a coming to terms of what is
and what will never be again...
Green is the color of rebirth
the yearning for change, to emerge
from this cathedral of pain
rise from the altar of hate...
Yellow is the color of hope
a belief in a tomorrow
to once again walk in the light...
Orange merges hope with frustration
as days become years
the rainbow bleeding into one
with an indomitable human spirit
to lift from the petri dish of turmoil
unfettered, free
to simply...be

HOPE

Hope is the prisoner who sits in a cell
believing that the sun will rise tomorrow
and that glint on barbed wire
will one day shine on him instead

Hope is looking beyond the immediate
the knowledge of a future
beyond the walls of confinement
to a world waiting...

Hope is the assurance that he can
pick up the pieces of a broken life
and find redemption in a new day
to live again-not as a number but as a person

Hope is like the air-invisible
yet fundamental to human life,
because without it, we are left to
struggle, gasping, against despair...

Song of the Prison Gate

The faces I have seen
passing through my portal
a descent into the maelstrom
Anger, fear, calculating eyes
as they shuffle by
becoming human compost
in a poisoned garden
Oh, the stories I could tell
of the many who pass by me
to sink into the quicksand
and mire, halcyon days gone
as they sit idle now
years and talents wasted
their pleas for mercy
and songs of innocence
to a blindfolded statue
that turns a deaf ear
as they wait on God

Who Am I?

Who am I?
>With this beard, itchy, unnatural
>because I am denied a razor
>arrayed in orange and white stripes
>looking like Garfield

Who am I?
>Confined to this cinderblock cell
>a window my only connection
>to a world I once knew, loved
>the rain washing the barbed-wire clean

Who am I?
>Staring at my watch
>as minutes slowly tick by
>is it meal time yet?
>I hope there are cookies

Who am I?
>My roommate snores
>as I stare into the darkness
>wondering, fearing
>is this how it feels in a coffin?

Gary K. Farlow

I Am Alive

I am

    evening shadows on the grass

    dew on a Morning Glory

    the crusty top of a snowfall

    the red sun of a hunter's dusk

    rustle of Autumn leaves

    crunch of a first frost

    glow of a full moon on a lake

    hazy heat of a Carolina summer

    wind proceeding a gentle rain

    fog on an August morning

I am

    Alive

GROUND ZERO

I had lived in dread of that late August

For as Whitman wrote

It was a year that trembled

and reeled beneath my feet...

Though that Summer was sultry

the air I breathed was out of January

my chills incongruent with the

molasses thick humidity

like a phantom before me...

I stood at a window of the courthouse

looking out upon the sorrowful entering...

I hear voices, uniting, rising in an anthem asking

Why is society not the one on trial?

For we who are awaiting judgement

shackled in chains

the song we sing is of memory

a mothers voice

the early morning smell in her kitchen

How many others in cells like mine

are awaiting the gavel's bang?

If justice be blind, then she is cruel

as I am just one out of millions...

America is either very, very cruel

Or the most evil people on the planet

Justice

Justice looks like many things
the freedom to talk back
the ability to find your voice
to ask hard questions
take a stand, for what you think is right
Our voice is our greatest power
to not be silenced when speaking out
For justice is a song we should all sing
from the streets of New York
to the dirt roads of Appalachia
justice belongs to everyone
For true justice is not justice
unless it is justice for all

PENITENT SNOW

Nature's shroud,
drapes the harsh angles
of man's inhumanity to man
softening the ugliness
bringing silence to chaos
stilling racing minds
harkening memories...
sodden mittens and hot cocoa
icicles suspended like prisms
cancelled school and snow cream...
Snow, feathery light
nature's paint over man's mistakes
and for just a moment
the world behind the wire
is just a bit more humane...

Gary K. Farlow

HOUSE OF TIME

Winter is the slayer of living things
the refrigerator of memories
Yet, hope still exists
even in the barren landscape of despair
In this place, a conspiracy of silence
one strives to heal a fractured heart
one beat at a time
For an environment cannot
determine your attitude,
but your attitude can
determine your environment
Triumph born of adversity
is the sweetest form of success
Should I grant control to the despair?
I must avoid bouts of moral self-pity,
as hope is the consultation of a weary traveler
whose destination cannot be seen
In this winter of my soul one learns
that loneliness is not an external phenomena
but internal, for you can be lonely in a crowd
Yet, spring will come
as sure as the rising sun--
freedom awaits

GARY K. FARLOW holds a Juris Doctorate from Thomas Jefferson College of Law at Heed University. He completed undergraduate studies at Western Illinois University. He is a two-time winner of the Pen America Writing Award for Prison Writers in 2002 and 2018.

His previous works include "Prisonese-A Survivor's Guide To Speaking Prison Slang," "The Cellblock Gourmet: Inmate Recipes From The Big House To Your House," "Doin' Time: How To Survive and Thrive In Prison," "Fragments of A Dream-The Poetry of Gary Farlow," "Porches, Puddin & Persimmons," and "The Warden, A Novel."

A.B.O. Comix is a collective of creators and activists who work to amplify the voices of LGBTQ prisoners through art. By working closely with prison abolitionist and queer advocacy organizations, we aim to keep queer prisoners connected to outside community and help them in the fight toward liberation. The profits we generate go back to incarcerated artists, especially those with little to no resources. Using the DIY ideology of "punk-zine" culture, A.B.O. was formed with the philosophy of mutual support, community and friendship.

Our collective is working towards compassionate accountability without relying on the state or its sycophants. A.B.O. believes our interpersonal and societal issues can be solved without locking people in cages. Our mission is to combat the culture that treats humans as disposable and disproportionately criminalizes the most marginalized amongst us. Through artistic activism, we hope to proliferate the idea that a better world means redefining our concepts of justice.

REFLECTIONS: